Fiddle Jam™

"A Way-Cool Easy Way to Learn How to Improvise!"

By Geoffrey Fitzhugh Perry

ISBN 0-634-04927-5

HAL•LEONARD®
CORPORATION

7777 W. BLUEMOUND RD. P.O. BOX 13819 MILWAUKEE, WI 53213

In Australia Contact:

Hal Leonard Australia Pty. Ltd.
22 Taunton Drive P.O. Box 5130
Cheltenham East, 3192 Victoria, Australia
Email: ausadmin@halleonard.com

Visit Hal Leonard Online at
www.halleonard.com

Welcome to Fiddle Jam!

Within these pages you'll find the stuff to introduce young (or at least young minded!) violinists to the joys of jamming to today's music in a fun and easy way, using the simplest possible fingerings so as to get to the point of non-thinking with maximum ease, developing a confident and authoritative connection between the creative mind, and the fingers at any level of technical development... and have *fun* while doing it!
Wow! Now that's one mouthful of a mission statement! ...

OK, now lets get started!!

Contents

THE INTRO SECTION

This is the **"Stuff"**: approach, attitude, philosophy, guidelines, use, etc…

Q & A's: A Few Things Before We Get Started

What is this book about? In short… **ATTITUDE.** This program is all about *doing* and not thinking, figuring, reading, or any other brain melting, creativity stopping activity (the notes will be drawn from inside your own mind).

Who is this book for? Anyone who plays, at any level, can benefit, but especially the near beginner who has just learned their first 2 or 3 open string-based major scales (G, D, and A major for violin; C, G, and D major for the viola and cello).

What can you expect to get out of this? The *"skinny"* answer is: a little knowledge, a little experience, some practical suggestions, a couple tunes, and hopefully lots of encouragement and smiles!

And the **"FAT"** answer: -You'll get direct experience at improvising in the "modern" forms of music which feature improvising as an important part of their style (like: rock, jazz, blues, cajun, country, and funk), knowledge of a variety of common keys and scales used for creating your own "solos;" through what I've called "EZ Zones" (symmetrically fingered patterns on two adjacent strings), some of the ins and outs of how this stuff works in the real world, and some general info and advise on the do's and don'ts for improvising.

Why is there (almost) no written music in this book?
Again, this program is all about creating, not duplicating someone else's ideas (though this is not completely harmful in balance. See * below). You will be training yourself to listen to and trust your own inner ideas and get them to your fingers. This is the most important skill we will be developing, as it seems to bring about many, so called, intangible benefits like: authority, confidence, relaxation, better musical phrasing (all of these, even when playing a *non*-improvised piece), and a host of others even beyond mere music (I find improvisers to be better problem solvers and creative thinkers in general). I believe this type of training is essential to musical development, and is sorely lacking in the traditional music education.

* note: I often find that fiddle jammers who use this program *do* sometimes subliminally pick up on the licks/riffs/ideas *I* played on the CD just by playing along. This is OK. It's a natural part of developing your jamming vocabulary.
See more about this subject on pages 58-60, "Obedience…"

What this book is NOT (I know that's not a question, but this isn't Jeopardy either!). Here's my answer: This book is NOT about bluegrass, country fiddling, Irish, Celtic, Scottish, or any other type of "traditional" fiddling tunes… there's already thousands of good books out on those styles.

This is all about doing your own thing, on the spot, off the cuff, faking it, winging it,… JAMMING!

How To Use This Book

#1 – RELAX, breathe deep (see page 15), and take your time. Hurrying, and its cousin worrying, are both counter-productive to creativity.

#2 – the basic idea is to use the notes from the fingering charts to play along with the corresponding cut on the CD, making up whatever YOU think sounds good while you listen and play.

#3 – "EZ-Zones" (which are simply symmetrical fingerings on two adjacent strings) are the best way I know to get started on the road to non-thinking (which is desirable for improvising). Just begin and end on a starred tonic note ("tonic" means the name of the key or scale), and you can't go wrong!

#4 – On the CD,**"Jam Stuff",** preceding each example, will guide you through a few musical ideas/riffs/licks/motifs to try.

#5 – Though the lessons in this program are designed in a particular *order* that coincides with a typical string player's development (major scales first, then EZ Zones fingering 0 1 3, then the tougher, 0 L2 3 fingerings, etc...), feel free to **try ANY lesson at ANY time.** I recommend scanning through the CD to find an example that appeals to you first and give it a whirl!

#6 – In each lesson, **"Preparation, Simple and Advanced Instructions, Listening Lessons, Troubleshooting, and P.J. (Post Jam)"** sections are there to further enhance the learning experience.

#7 – *"Wit and Wisdom"* pages are scattered throughout the book. They are like musician's life lesson stories and are there for your information (and hopefully enlightenment), giving you further jam stuff to chew on.

Violin Fingering Chart and Ledger

Beginner's tape marks are represented by white horizontal lines. (Dark horizontal line at top = instrument's nut). Finger numbers are in columns on either side of chart and strings (vertical lines) are left to right, low to high.

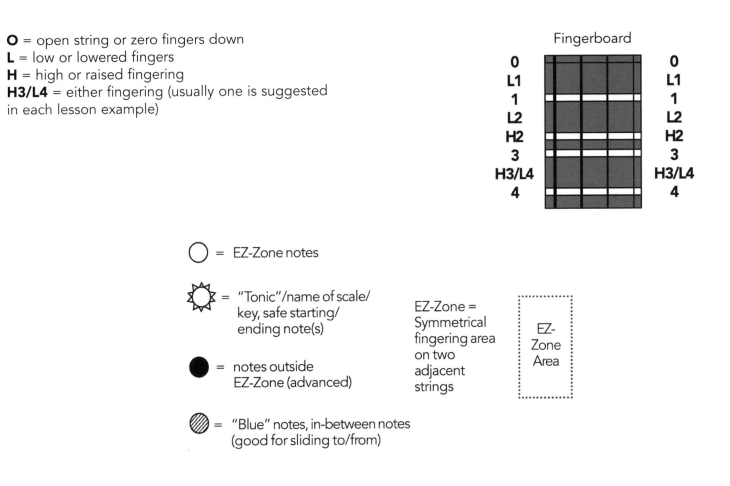

O = open string or zero fingers down
L = low or lowered fingers
H = high or raised fingering
H3/L4 = either fingering (usually one is suggested in each lesson example)

Fingerboard

0				0
L1				L1
1				1
L2				L2
H2				H2
3				3
H3/L4				H3/L4
4				4

◯ = EZ-Zone notes

☀ = "Tonic"/name of scale/ key, safe starting/ ending note(s)

● = notes outside EZ-Zone (advanced)

◙ = "Blue" notes, in-between notes (good for sliding to/from)

EZ-Zone = Symmetrical fingering area on two adjacent strings

EZ-Zone Area

Viola Scale Fingering Adaptation Charts

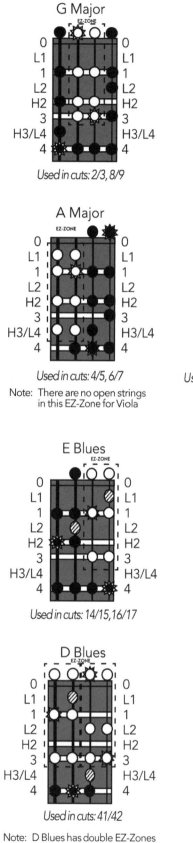

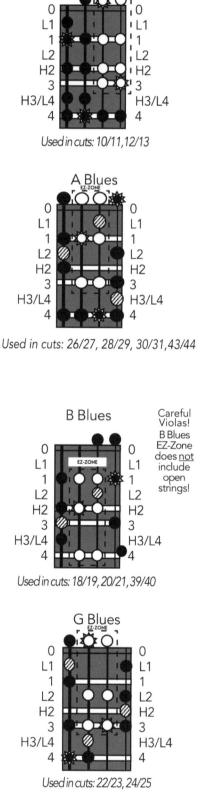

G Major
Used in cuts: 2/3, 8/9

D Major
Used in cuts: 10/11,12/13

A Major
Used in cuts: 4/5, 6/7

Note: There are no open strings
in this EZ-Zone for Viola

A Blues
Used in cuts: 26/27, 28/29, 30/31,43/44

E Blues
Used in cuts: 14/15,16/17

B Blues
Used in cuts: 18/19, 20/21,39/40

Careful
Violas!
B Blues
EZ-Zone
does not
include
open
strings!

D Blues
Used in cuts: 41/42

G Blues
Used in cuts: 22/23, 24/25

Note: D Blues has double EZ-Zones

Cello Scale Fingering Adaptation Charts

G Major

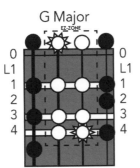

Used in cuts: 2/3, 8/9

D Major

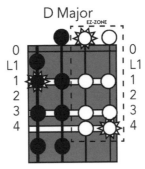

Used in cuts: 10/11, 12/13

A Major

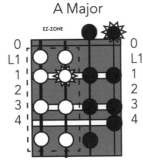

Used in cuts: 4/5,6/7

Note: There are no open strings in this EZ-Zone for Cellos!

A Blues

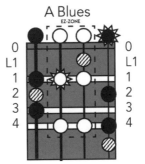

Used in cuts: 26/27,28/29,30/31,43/44

E Blues

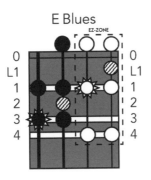

Used in cuts: 14/15, 16/17

B Blues

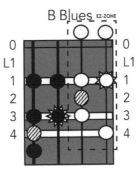

Used in cuts: 18/19, 20/21, 39/40

G Blues

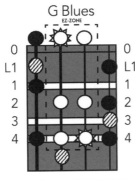

Used in cuts: 22/23, 24/25

D Blues

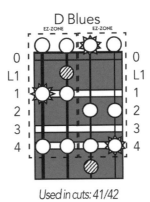

Used in cuts: 41/42

Note: D Blues has a double EZ-Zone.

About My Performances on This CD...

I had a tough task. Here I am, promoting a non-thinking creative approach to improvising, yet found myself in the position of having to *think!* It is something I've become rather unaccustomed to – thankfully, but I thought it important to try and play within the EZ Zones only (or close to it) for the beginning of each example, *then* get free-er later in the example, using the extended scale notes, to show the possibilities.

So, to my ears, I sound a bit stiff at first, but that's only because I was doing what I am telling you *NOT* to! Which is: *THINK!*

In general, I tried to keep all the performances, on all the instruments, in sync with the overall attitude of this method – that of: GO FOR IT, DON'T THINK, JUST DO. All performances you hear are 1st or 2nd takes (and 2nd, only if there was a blatant mistake). None are perfect. ...and that is beautiful and perfect in it's own way. I left it as is, warts and all, because that's the way it is in "real" life – **live, spontaneous, and in the moment.**

"In the Studio"

Photo image by Dan Syracuse/Big Bang Graphics

"A Sound Environment"

Rock 'n' Roll has a reputation for being loud and obnoxious. It's a beautiful thing in my opinion. Joyous and unafraid. Historically I believe this approach came largely from a post-World War II overall American attitude of, "we are the greatest, strongest, and most victorious nation on earth!," which has pervaded nearly all music since. Now I'm not trying to cultivate hearing damaged rock n roll kids (I know that standing next to loud drummers and electric guitarists in mostly small clubs has taken its toll on my own hearing – I've worn ear plugs for 10 of my 20 years as a professional in an attempt to ward of any further damage), but there needs to be a healthy security blanket of volume surrounding an improviser.

Listening level is critical. Too quiet can lead to self-consciousness (not good), or lack of control (for trying to play overly soft to match CD), and can thwart the development of the ability to listen to self and others *EQUALLY.* The old report card comment of, "plays well with others" is really *really* important here! The volume of the accompanying music needs to be the same as the improviser's own instrument at *their* ears so they're not holding back (or "a bit louder than," is OK too when just getting used to all this – remember, I said "security blanket").

With acoustic instruments, we're not talking about ear splitting volume either, but if the noise (a matter of opinion of course, but especially "rock 'n' roll" noise) is too much for neighbors, there are numerous options including: personal headphones, instrument mutes (combined with turning the CD player down to match), and as of this writing, a "silent" electric practice violin being marketed by Yamaha (www.yamaha.com), in which you can listen to yourself in headphones along with an input from a CD player (a cool idea other manufacturers should be quick to pick up on). There's no sense in torturing your neighbors (even if you'd like to). To do so would probably just distract you from the "real deal" of learning to consistently listen to you own inner ideas. **Balance** is the name of this game.

The Good Soil

Creativity is a brain muscle to be flexed and strengthened every day. Children are naturally free and creative, but it is also well documented that by the age of 8 or 9 (the usual age they start playing in school), they are well on their way to having their natural creative urges *squashed!*

Children are probably the most fertile ground we have on this planet. Plant the seeds. Self esteem, confidence, trust, authority, obedience, concentration, relaxation, are just some of the positive words that come up because of improvisation. There is mounting evidence that improvising actually enhances neurological growth in certain parts of the brain (and that's a *permanent* benefit!). Therapy, healing, attention disorders, mood enhancement, just keeping a kid interested rather than quitting is worth the try.

My Motto:

"Start 'em young and put smiles on their faces."

...and, of course, I could, but *need* I say more?

THE MAJOR SCALE SECTION

Most beginning violin students already know a major scale or two. It's one of the first things we learn after Twinkle Twinkle Little Star, Hot Cross Buns, and Mary Had a Little Lamb, or other such songs. Major scales are very wholesome and familiar sounding. You've probably heard the notes sung as Do, Re, Mi, Fa, So, La, Ti, Do, at one time or another.

Major scales are called "Major" because they're a really *BIG DEAL*. Most things you learn about music will be based on them. Many think the scale is a bit too sweet and plain sounding for rock n roll, but you'll be able to do some cool things with it playing to these examples.

The Raven's Daughter

She's a rockin' in the topper-most pop!

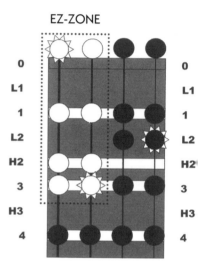

Jam Stuff: Cut 2

Jam Example: Cut 3

Bird Seed: Familiar folk-rock.

Scale/Key: G Major.

Notes: any, G, A, B, C, D, E, or F#'s.

EZ-Zone: 0, 1, h2, 3, on the G and D strings.

Scale Character: Wholesome, pure and strong.

Preparation: Run the EZ-Zone notes up and down, then twist them up a bit, skip around, and get free with it until un-thinking.

Instructions:
Simple: Start and end on a G. Stay within the EZ-Zone and you can't go wrong! Remember, it's *your* creation, so play whatever YOU feel sounds good.

Advanced: See/hear "Jam Stuff" on the CD for an idea or two. Travel outside the EZ-Zone a bit. Try skipping the C's and F#'s more (this is called a Major Pentatonic scale - more on that later). Oh yeah, and don't be afraid to get a little intense about it.

Listening Lesson: Notice how this one's basically a repeated guitar riff with one different section (a C chord) that "turns it around" back to the top. Can you find/hear it? Try playing some things during this section that will contrast with the repeated riff section (like: a more choppy or smooth rhythm, or a different speed to your notes, etc...). Also notice how this cut ends on the C chord as opposed to a G chord (called the tonic chord in this key) for a little added mystery and suspense.

Troubleshooting: Don't play too much! Leave some room for it to "breathe"... just like a singer.

★ ★ ★ ★ ★

P.J. (Post Jam): Tell yourself (or have someone else tell you) that you are the sassiest fiddler in the modern world for what you just improvised to this track!

Le Bomb

...get into the mood, it's a party!

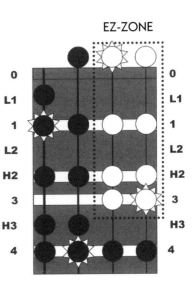

EZ-ZONE

Jam Stuff: Cut 4

Jam Example: Cut 5

Lighting the Fuse: A french twist to an American standard.

Scale: A Major.

Notes: any A,B,C#,D,E,F#, or G#.

EZ-Zone: 0, 1, h2, 3, on A and E strings.

Scale Character: Bright, happy, sweet.

Preparation: Run the scale up, down, skipping, hopping, jumping, running, crawling, etc... until fairly un-thinking.

Instructions:

Simple: Use EZ-Zone notes any way YOU think sounds good with the cut. Start and end on an A, and you can't go wrong.

Advanced: Check out "Jam Stuff" for an idea. Be consistently aware of "hearing" what you want to play before you play it.

Listening Lesson: This example is basically a 2 measure repeated idea with a 4 measure "turnaround" section (E chord) which leads it back to the basic "riff." Imagine the 2 measure riff during the drum break too. Can you "hear" it?

Troubleshooting: Keep it moving on this one, but not far, as you're never more that a note or two away from a more desirable note if you don't like the one you're on.

★ ★ ★ ★ ★

P.J. (Post Jam): Scrinkle up your nose and tell yourself, "you don't know what you're doing!"... then laugh out loud and say, "of course not! This is IMPROVISING, except for knowing the scale, my mind is perfectly *empty!*"

"Violin vs. Fiddle"

"If I had a nickel for every time someone asked me..."

What's the difference between a fiddle and a violin? *NONE*. Same instrument, different names for different occasions. I'm told that at one time in musical instrument history (more than 400 years ago) there *were* two separate families of bowed stringed instruments: viols and fiddles. But, ever since the so called perfection of the instrument's design in the early 1700's by the likes of Antonius Stradivarius (whose name is today a household term meaning "of the top-most quality"), the name debate has raged.

Today, "violin" is the official and legitimate name for the instrument, and "fiddle", is the affectionate/fun/slang term for the same instrument. Fiddle is more often used when connected to certain kinds of popular music like country, bluegrass, and cajun especially, but in general, anything non-classical. As an example, the jamming in this program definitely falls into the fiddle world, but in reality, there is no difference at all.

"Violin vs. Fiddle"
"the ying and yang of tradition broken"

Stradivarius copy and five string Aceto Violect "moderne" model
by Ithaca Stringed Instruments.
Photo image by Dan Syracuse/Big Bang Graphics.

Spiral Travels

Round and round goes the familiar sound!

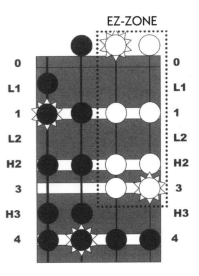

EZ-ZONE

Jam Stuff: Cut 6

Jam Example: Cut 7

Full Circle: a repetitive, but famous chord progression put to a rock beat.

Scale: A Major.

Notes: any, A, B, C#, D, E, F#, or G#'s.

EZ-Zone: 0, 1, h2, 3, on the A and E strings.

Scale Character: Happy, bright, and *"in."*

Preparation: Run the EZ-Zone notes all around, and up and down (until fairly un-thinking of course!).

Instructions:
Simple: Start and end on an A, stay within the EZ-Zone, and you can't go wrong! Remember, it's your creation, so play whatever YOU feel will sound good with the cut.

Advanced: See/hear "Jam Stuff" on the CD for an idea or two. Expand to scale notes outside the EZ-Zone.

Listening Lesson: Notice how, even though the major scale is normally bright, happy, and almost too sweet sounding, that it still can sound rockin' with the right attitude and accompaniment.

Troubleshooting: Remember that, if you don't like the sound of a note you are on, you are never more than a half or whole step (fingers close or spaced respectively) from a note that will fit the chord quite nicely. Don't think about it too much, just keep it light and moving on this one.

★ ★ ★ ★ ★

P.J. (Post Jam): Tell yourself (or have someone *else* tell you) that you are the popper-most of the topper-most and your improv is so good that you can run around with the big boys!

The Rarest Rose

It's philosophical, but true, we must take the time to smell this most delicate aroma.

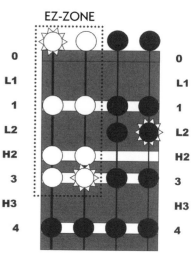

Jam Stuff: Cut 8

Jam Example: Cut 9

Aromatherapy: the beauty of the Ballad.

Scale/Key: G Major.

Notes: any, G, A, B, C, D, E, or F#'s.

EZ-Zone: 0, 1, h2, 3, on the G and D strings.

Scale Character: Smooth, sweet and right.

Preparation: Run the EZ-Zone to warm your ears up to it, breathe deep, loosen up, and get your mind ready to listen and respond.

Instructions:

Simple: Start and end on a G. Stay within the EZ-Zone and you can't go wrong! Remember, it's _your_ creation, so play whatever _YOU_ feel sounds good as you respond to the cut.

Advanced: See/hear "Jam Stuff" on the CD for an idea or two. Try to hear what you'd like to play _further_ ahead of time (at least a measure). There's plenty of time in the ballad style – take it. Developing this internal listening ability is _"THE"_ skill to have and a measure of true greatness (*see page 25).

Listening Lesson: Listen to the chord progression. Can you hear where it is headed? Can you tell when it starts again? There is a middle "B" section in this example, can you find/hear it?

Troubleshooting: Don't trick yourself into thinking that what you play has to be the most amazingly beautiful thing you've ever heard. Playing _anything_ to a beautiful background such as this will make you sound great! Relax, keep it simple, use lots of bow, but lightly, to help your tone be big and fat, yet a bit airy too, always concentrating within to find your best ideas.

★ ★ ★ ★ ★

P.J. (Post Jam): Tell yourself (or have someone else tell you – and they really might mean it, you know!) that what you just improvised was so _beautiful_ that even the _angels_ were smiling!

14

"Oh Yeah... and Don't Forget to Breathe!"

As odd as this sounds, you'd be surprised at how many people stop breathing unconsciously, or even hold their breath on purpose when trying to concentrate. Breathing is probably the most important and necessary thing you can do. It's the first and the last thing you will do as a human being on this planet and essential to life, health, concentration, and relaxation. Did I succeed at making it sound like a big deal? I hope so.

At one time or another all my students get the "breathing speech," and I ask them:

1) "How long can you live without *food*?" Their answers vary (some think only to lunch, others maybe one day or two max...), but the truth is, depending on how fat you are, roughly around one month.

2) "How long can you go without *sleep*?" Again, answers vary, but sleep deprivation experiments usually last less than one week to the best of my knowledge (until the subject falls into some sort of sleep coma!).

3) "How long can you go without water?" Dying of dehydration can happen in a matter of 3 or 4 days, of course, depending on how much you sweat!

And finally,

4) "How long can you go without air?" Not months, not weeks, not days, not hours, not even a few minutes before brain damage occurs!!! It is in everyone's best interest to breathe deep full breaths, just as babies do naturally, and singers, martial artists, and athletes (to name a few) are trained to do. Oxygen is direct brain fuel. Relaxed concentration and good memory (along with a strong immune system and a host of other benefits) can not be had without it.

Try this:

Breathe in though your nose, pretending your stomach is a balloon, and you are filling it with air, extending your stomach outward as you breathe in, and then breathe out through your mouth, deflating the balloon (your stomach) completely. Do this a few times a day at least. Try it before any task – like improvising – and see if you don't notice a clearer mind and better concentration along with benefits like more control, relaxation, and even endurance! Making this a regular part of your life will make you a better student and could change your life – literally!

It has mine.

Cajun Waltz

In the mood? Care to dance? It's a tradition!

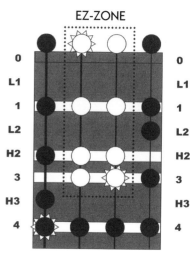

Jam Stuff: Cut 10

Jam Example: Cut 11

In Step: a simple three-beater with a little spicy sizzle.

Scale/Key: D Major.

Notes: any, D, E, F#, G, A, B, and C#'s.

EZ-Zone: 0, 1, h2, 3, on D and A strings.

Scale Character: Sweet, happy and satisfed

Preparation: Run the EZ- Zone notes up and down, sideways, diagonal, random, etc...until fairly un-thinking.

Instructions:

Simple: Start and end on a D, use the EZ-Zone, and play whatever _YOU_ feel sounds good – remember, it's _your_ creation, so you can't go wrong!

Advanced: See/hear "Jam Stuff" on the CD. Try to create a smooth melody, "hear" it ahead of time in your mind. Go with the dynamics of the track. Pretend you're in a blissful trance-like reverie.

Listening Lesson: Notice that I "walk" up to G at the beginning (G is the first chord in this example, not D as usual for this key).

Troubleshooting: Sounding extra simple is extra OK here. Use lots of bow and some vibrato on select long notes if you can.

★ ★ ★ ★ ★

P.J. (Post Jam): Tell yourself (or have someone else tell you) that was so beautiful it made all the ladies (and even some of the _guys_) cry!

Contra Dance

Line up with your partners now, it's plain and simple.

Jam Stuff: Cut 12

Jam Example: Cut 13

The Ancestral Call: Ancient origins from a time of olde.

Scale/Key: D Major.

Notes: any, D, E, F#, G, A, B, and C#'s.

EZ-Zone: 0, 1, h2, 3, on the D and A strings.

Scale Character: sweet, plain, and right.

Preparation: Run the EZ-Zone notes to warm your ears to the sound of the scale, and noodle around with it a bit.

Instructions:

Simple: Start and end on a D. Use the EZ-Zone to play whatever _YOU_ feel sounds good. Remember, it's _your_ creation, you can't go wrong!

Advanced: See/hear "Jam Stuff" on the CD. Listen for _your_ notes in _your_ mind just before you play them. Train yourself to trust these inner ideas and copy them, they're yours after all, and it's OK! If you're having trouble with this, try to copy what I played at first until you get the hang of the concept.

Listening Lesson: Even though there's not an obvious drum beat in this cut (like in a rock tune for example), listen for the steady down and up motion of the rhythm. Train yourself to mentally "lock in" with what musicians call the "back beat" (an accent, usually on the snare drum, on beats 2 and 4 of each measure, in a 4 beat meter). Learn to feel this even when it's not right "in your face."

Troubleshooting: Keep it ultra-simple on this one. Try to "place" each note exactly where you want it. Keep the word "corny" in mind. Doing this helped me to get better at "playing on purpose," and have more fun while doing so!

★ ★ ★ ★ ★

P.J. (Post Jam): Tell yourself (or have someone else tell you) how wonderful you just did. You really are the nice boy (or girl) your Mama always wanted you to be! :)

"Blues Attitude"

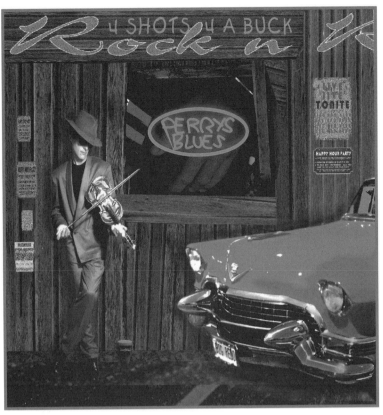

Photo image by Dan Syracuse/Big Bang Graphics

and now for the really cool stuff...
The 0 1 3 Blues Scale Section

I would've put this chapter first, but skipping fingers is sometimes a technical hang-up for those just starting out. Nevertheless, I find that students quickly acclimate to skipping the second finger with a little preperatory practice. Many may find it even easier than major and definitely easier to get to the non-thinking state. Just remember that this is a "less is more" kind of scale, so be prepared to keep it simple and have some FUN!

E Funki

eewww... sounds like a bad Bacteria!

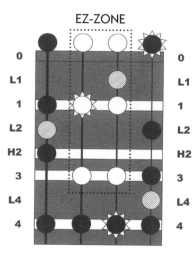

Jam Stuff: Cut 14

Jam Example: Cut 15

The Nitti-Gritti: Get down and get dirty, down to the funky roots of rock n roll!

Scale: E Blues (minor pentatonic).

Notes: any E, G, A, B, and D (with B♭'s thrown in for some sizzle).

EZ-Zone: 0,1,3, on D and A strings.

Scale Character: Bold and clashing, but cool.

Preparation: Practice the EZ-Zone notes any/every way: up, down, sideways, skipping, hopping, running, random... you get the idea, just get it to the point that it becomes a "no-brainer!"

Instructions:

Simple: Use the EZ-Zone, start and end on an E, and you can't go wrong. Remember, it's your creation, so play whatever *YOU* feel will sound good with the cut.

Advanced: See/hear "Jam Stuff" on the CD for an idea or two. Using *any* EGABD, expand to scale notes outside the EZ-Zone. Start by adding 4th finger notes and sliding into the B's.

Troubleshooting: Keep it rhythmical and simple. Don't think, just do.

P.J. (Post Jam): Tell yourself (or have some else tell you), for what we just heard you improvise, you are the *baddest* fiddle funkster to ever set foot on a stage (even if it's just your bedroom)!

E12

Like Vitamin B12, it's essential to a healthy rock n roll vocabulary!

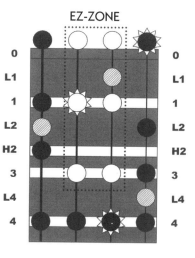

Jam Stuff: Cut 16

Jam Example: Cut 17

Just Enuff: It's a 12 bar Blues plain and simple.

Scale/Key: E Blues.

Notes: any, E, G, A, B, or D's (plus B♭'s as an extra note if you feel like it).

EZ-Zone: 0, 1, 3, on the D and A strings.

Scale Character: Rootsy, earthy, guttural, a little mean and nasty (in a fun sort of way).

Preparation: Get comfortable, and agile as possible with the EZ-Zone notes. In other words, just get ready to **let it RIP!** Don't think, just do.

Instructions:

Simple: Start and end on an E. Stay within the EZ-Zone and you can't go wrong! Remember, it's *your* creation, so play whatever *YOU* feel sounds good.

Advanced: See/hear "Jam Stuff" on the CD for an idea or two. Slide B♭'s up to B's. Expand to other scale notes outside the Zone (start by adding open E). Let your notes and rhythms be like an imaginary conversation.

Listening Lesson: Learn to feel when the 12 bar phrase repeats. Let the awareness of this become second nature to you.

Troubleshooting: Keep it simple at first. Don't be afraid to repeat notes... even one over and over! Have fun with it.

P.J. (Post Jam): Tell yourself (or have someone else tell you) that you were just simply the "baddest!" Go ahead, look in the mirror and tell yourself so!

"Strike of the Sword"

Photo image by Dan Syracuse/Big Bang Graphics

"Play What You Are"

In the "Now"
One of the beauties of improvising is that it is never the same twice and can also change with our ever changing moods. Feeling angry today? Play loud and choppy. Attack each new note like the strike of a sword! Anger is a _BIG_ element of rock n roll. Feeling mellow? Pick a major scale example and play sweet and easy using lots of bow and slurs. Not feeling any particular mood? Challenge yourself and pretend that you are! Just as an actor would, learn to play an emotion on command.

Individuality
Each person has their own distinct personality that comes into play when improvising. Are you generally outgoing? Shy? Fiery? Happy? Let a piece (at least) of your true self shine through and color whatever you improvise.

Take what's Given
A good improviser will play to the mood of the song too... new song, new mood. Just listen, feel, and respond.

B Tuff

Get down and get funky to the bottoms of your platform shoes!...
I'll bet you didn't think a violin could do that.

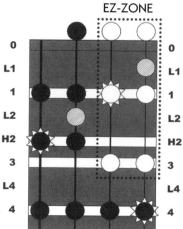

Jam Stuff: Cut 18

Jam Example: Cut 19

The Funk: Macho Man has come to jam!

Scale: B Blues.

Key: B "universal" (minor notes in the scale mixed with major notes in the chords).

Notes: any, B, D, E, F#, or A (with F naturals thrown in at your discretion).

EZ-Zone: 0, 1, 3, on the A and E strings.

Scale Character: Brash, Clashing, but way-cool.

Preparation: Run the EZ-Zone notes any-which-way until fairly un-thinking.

Instructions:

Simple: Start and end on a B. Stay within the EZ-Zone and you can't go wrong! Remember, it's _your_ creation, so play whatever _YOU_ feel sounds good.

Advanced: See/hear "Jam Stuff" on the CD for an idea or two. Expand to notes outside the EZ-Zone and try sliding into the F#'s from the F naturals.

Listening Lesson: Listen to the funky guitar chord (B7+9). It has both major _and_ minor notes in it simultaneously and is the embodiment of the clashing, but glorious, funky/bluesy sound.

Troubleshooting: Don't be shy on this one. Pretend you have a black leather motorcycle jacket on (if you don't already), un-zipped of course. Don't be afraid to take some chances and get a little _noisy_ even. It's OK, you have my permission... really!

★ ★ ★ ★ ★

P.J. (Post Jam): Tell yourself (or have someone else tell you) that you are the _baddest_ in the fiddlin' land for what you just jammed to this cut!

B GONE

You're gonna regret your mistreatin' ways.

Jam Stuff: Cut 20

Jam Example: Cut 21

In the Mood: A serious minor blues.

Scale: B Blues.

Key: B minor.

Notes: any, B, D, E, F#, or A (with some F naturals thrown in for fun too).

EZ-Zone: 0, 1, 3, on the A and E strings.

Scale Character: "I'm feeling bad, but-isn't-that-a-wonderful-and beautiful-part-of-life-we-all-share-sometimes" kind of feeling.

Preparation: Run the EZ-Zone notes up, down, inside out and backwards until about un-thinking.

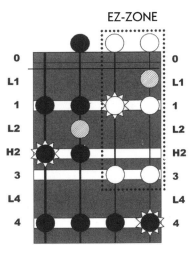

EZ-ZONE

Instructions:

<u>Simple:</u> Start and end on a B. Stay within the EZ-Zone and you can't go wrong! Remember, it's *your* creation, so play whatever *YOU* feel sounds good.

<u>Advanced:</u> See/hear "Jam Stuff" on the CD for an idea or two. Expand to notes outside the EZ-Zone, and slide into the F#'s from the F naturals.

Listening Lesson: In a longer sense, learn to *feel* the length of the 12 bar phrase, *without* counting. Listen internally. Can you *hear* it coming before you actually get there?

Troubleshooting: Play each note on *purpose*. I know that this sounds extra dumb, but it's harder to do *consistently* than you might think! Don't let your fingers tell <u>you</u> what to play, you tell <u>them</u> what to play, because your ideas come from a higher source of authority - the depths of your *soul*, the universal collective consciousness of all musical ideas...or something like that. Ha!

P.J. (Post Jam): Tell yourself (or have someone else tell you) that you've got the blues to bottom of your soles (of your shoes that is, at least! Ha!), and what you just improvised to this cut was a mirror for all people who have ever felt hurt or oppressed, and now they are all healed because of *you*...their blues savior!!

"Mary and the Rhythm Kings"

Imagine this...

You've just learned your first big song, "Mary Had a Little Lamb." You go home, all excited, to play it for your Mom. You play all the correct notes, in the correct order, with beautiful tone, but with no regard to the length of each note (go ahead, try this!). The result is barely recognizable!

A good mom would probably smile, pat you on the head, tell you, "that's nice," and encourage you to keep practicing (but probably thinking: "Man, this kid just doesn't have *it*.")

OK, now imagine a different scene...

You've learned the same song, and run home to show Mom, but in your sugared-up, hyperactive excitement, *forgot* the correct notes! Oh well, eager for praise, you're determined to play it anyways. Singing the song in your mind, you play all the *wrong* notes, but, in the exact rhythm of "Mary Had a Little Lamb" at least (try this on your violin or by banging your fists in random clusters of notes on a piano to the song's rhythm and you should get the idea).

Which version is more recognizable as the song? I haven't met a single person who, having heard both examples, doesn't think the second (correct rhythm, wrong notes) is the more recognizable of the two.

...and the moral of the story?

Rhythm Is Always King.

Why?...

Again, I'll ask: Why?

Beats Me! (pun *intended.* Ha!). Human beings just seem to latch on to rhythm easier than pitch. Maybe it's because of our caveman - banging on drum - past? Who knows?! It just is.

Obviously, *BOTH* correct notes *and* correct rhythm *together* is best, but, if in performance, you must choose, you are better off to play a wrong note at the right time. I'll bet the majority of your audience either won't even know the difference, or will be at least very forgiving.

How does this concept effect the improviser?

Don't *worry* about the right notes so much*... remember, it's *your* creation, you can do anything you want to ultimately. A single note played in a cool rhythm, can be just as exciting as a fast flourish of notes. My advise (especially if just starting): GO FOR *RHYTHM* FIRST.

*(see #1 in "How to Use This Book" on page 5)

The 0, L2, 3 SECTION

Some think this EZ-Zone is even easier than Major and the 0, 1, 3 blues scale examples. After getting used to skipping the first finger (admittedly an odd sensation at first), it feels very fundamentally "grounded" to put the tonic note on an open string (like our Major scale examples), but also still fun and rebellious like the minor pentatonic/blues scale that it is.

G SWING

Holy cherry poppin' squirrel nuts Batman, it's like the latest cool craze!

Jam Stuff: Cut 22

Jam Example: Cut 23

In the Groove: 12 bar blues with a swing beat and "walking" bass.

Scale: G Blues.

Key: G "universal" (mixed minor notes from the blues scale and major notes in the chords).

Notes: any, G, B♭, C, D, or F (with D♭'s thrown in for some color).

EZ-Zone: 0, L2, 3, on the G and D strings.

Scale Character: Hip cool jazzy/bluesy with pleasing clashes between the "blue" notes of the scale (like: B♭ and D♭) and major notes which build the chords.

Preparation: Run the EZ-Zone notes any which way until fairly un-thinking.

Instructions:
Simple: Start and end on a G. Stay within the EZ-Zone and you can't go wrong! Remember, it's your creation, so play whatever YOU feel sounds good.

Advanced: See/hear "Jam Stuff" on the CD for an idea or two. Expand to the scale notes outside the EZ-Zone. Include some D♭'s and slide up to your D's.

Listening Lesson: Tune your attention onto the Bass and how it continually leads you from chord to chord, and then notice how the cymbals "ride" the rhythm with a slight accent on beats 2 and 4.

Troubleshooting: So called _trained_ violinists are notorious for sounding too stiff on swing rhythms. Relax, keep it light, loose, and more liquid-y, always feeling the first and third triplet of each beat. It will probably feel the most natural to use a down bow on the down beat, and a quick (but light) up bow on the third of the triplets. If that's still not helping, try pretending that you are lazy, tired, or even _drunk_ for a while!

★ ★ ★ ★ ★

P.J. (Post Jam): Tell yourself (or have someone else tell you) that you are the hippest cat ever to arch their back for playing what you just did!

MOON DIGGIN'

It's music to strip mine too!

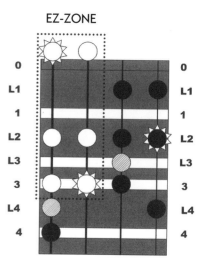

EZ-ZONE

Jam Stuff: Cut 24

Jam Example: Cut 25

The Blast Off: Fun, pop rock, medium tempo.

Scale: G Blues.

Key: G minor.

Notes: any, G, B♭, C, D, or F (and some D♭'s thrown in for fun).

EZ-Zone: 0, L2, 3, on the G and D strings.

Scale Character: Poking, prodding, and invasive, but still "in."

Preparation: Go *nuts* within the EZ-Zone until fairly un-thinking.

Instructions:

Simple: Start and end on a G. Stay within the EZ-Zone and you can't go wrong! Remember, it's *your* creation, so play whatever *YOU* feel sounds good.

Advanced: See/hear "Jam Stuff" on the CD for an idea or two. Expand to notes outside the EZ-Zone. Add some D♭'s, and slide into your D's.

Listening Lesson: Listen to the cut *without* playing (preferably with your eyes closed) and imagine yourself standing on a stage in front of a large crowd playing what *you'd* like to hear... then go back, and listen again, only this time improvise along, playing as close as you can to what you just imagined.

Troubleshooting: Skipping the 1st finger (as you do in this EZ-Zone) is something some people have trouble with at first. Make sure to pay special attention to the intonation of your L2nd finger, as it is critical to the sound and feeling of this scale. If your fingers are in tune, playing this sequence of notes: B♭, G, B♭, G, B♭, B♭, G, C, B♭, G, should sound like the familiar tune children (and some times grown-ups!) sing to each other when they are trying to taunt them into a "na na, you can't get me" kind of chase. Can you hear it? That is the sound (and probably the *feeling* too) needed for this example. Other than that: don't think, be bold, and have some rhythmic fun!

★ ★ ★ ★ ★

P.J. (Post Jam): Tell yourself (or have someone else tell you) that you are the most talented and amazing creator ever to touch a violin (or *your* violin, at least!), and are destined for fame and fortune!

"Master Zhu"
"Levitating while receiving cosmically channelled alien musical ideas,
and reeling in his audience with appropriately frosted cake!"

Photo image by Dan Syracuse/Big Bang Graphics

<u>*Wit & Wisdom*</u>

OBEDIENCE TO THE MASTER, GREATNESS, and SHOWING OFF

The ultimate and lofty goal of an improviser (and possibly anyone in any place or discipline!), is to be a complete and undistorted mirror of your own creative innermost promptings (please notice I said "creative" and not *destructive promptings,* as I'm not trying to develop self-serving idiots, smashing violins over each others heads and poking each other in the eye with their bow tips, just because some inner "voice" told them to do so! Ha!).

Greatness as an improviser, actually has *nothing* to do with technique. ...But has *everything* to do with these promptings and the ability to be completely connected from your "inner ear" to your finger tips. This is what really matters most.

Music is a *service* to the listener and the player ultimately is just a channel for ideas. Where these ideas come from, who knows... might be God or angels, your imagination, space alien telepathy, the collective possibilities of all notes you've ever heard and/or played, or maybe "all of the above" (and I'd bet on the later... *including* the space aliens!).

The Bottom Line is we don't really know for sure, but this I do know: good things come from learning to trust and be obedient to "it," and misery and disappointment come when we are not.

Hook, line, and sinker, reeling in your audience.

Now, no matter how connected to the divine muses we become, I personally still leave room for around 10% of showing off! People seem to like it and remember you for it. I find that most people aren't really on the lookout for notes of divine beauty at first and sometimes need a little "flash" to grab their attention. Cake is OK, but cake with *frosting* is *way* better (but only as long as there is not *too* much frosting, of course!).

THE A BLUES COMBINATION "EZ-ZONE" SECTION

Check it out! The A Blues scale has *two*, yes count 'em, two (2) EZ-Zones on the violin! 0, 1, 3, on the G and D strings, *and*, 0, L2, 3, on the A and E strings. Of course, this is improvising, so you can do anything you want with them (see * below), but the flowing combination of the two will help you to sound "most masterful" over these examples.

*Re: "anything you want," including staying within just one of the "zones", staying on just one string, one note, or, I suppose, no notes at all if you so choose! - though I don't recommend that. Silence is "golden" and a necessary part of music of course, but let's say that you have to play at least one note for it to be improvising. OK?

A POTTER'S WHEEL

Yes, Rock can be shaped and spun by nice folk like you and me too!

Jam Stuff: Cut 26

Jam Example: Cut 27

The Molding Material: Light rock.

Scale: A Blues.

Key: A minor.

Notes: any, A, C, D, E, or G (with some E♭'s thrown in for color).

EZ-Zones: *Low:* 0, 1, 3, on the G and D strings, and/or,
High: 0, L2, 3, on the A and E strings.

Scale Character: Like a good party joke: funny, interesting, and a bit off color now and then.

Preparation: Run the EZ-Zone notes separately until fairly un-thinking, then together, top to bottom.

Instructions:

Simple: Start and end on an A. Stay within the EZ-Zones and you can't go wrong! Remember, it's *your* creation, so play whatever *YOU* feel will sound good.

Advanced: See/hear "Jam Stuff" on the CD for an idea or two. Add E♭'s and slide into your E's. Try to visualize the combined EZ-Zones as a fingerboard s*hape.*

Listening Lesson: Notice the happy bounciness to this cut and then try to mirror that in your playing.

Troubleshooting: No need to run the length of the combined EZ-Zones all at once. There's no harm in taking your time and staying in one area for a while, moving higher or lower in support of some dynamic contrast. To get the hang of this, experiment with staying in a very small area (like only two or three notes on one string) to see how much variety you can squeeze out of it.

Also, work on connecting the two EZ-Zones seamlessly by practicing the transition from the D string to the A string only, for a bit.

★ ★ ★ ★ ★

P.J. (Post Jam): Tell yourself (or have someone else tell you) that what you just improvised was simply the sweetest thing... like *ear* candy!

BLUE SUIT in a ROADHOUSE BAR of 12

Standing out with the rough crowd.

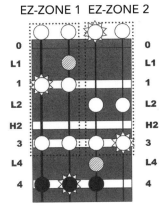

Jam Stuff: Cut 28

Jam Example: Cut 29

The Jump Start: Cool, blue, straight forward and easy. Blues like it wants to be.

Scale: A Blues.

Key: A "universal" (a mix of minor notes in the scale and major notes in the chords).

Notes: Any, A, C, D, E, or G (with E♭'s thrown in for some fun).

EZ-Zones: *Low:* 0, 1, 3, on the G and D strings, *and/or High:* 0, L2, 3, on the A and E strings.

Scale Character: Wailing, whining, crying, and a little angry, but glad to be alive.

Preparation: Run the EZ-Zone notes from top to bottom, sideways, diagonal, etc.... until you start dreaming of them at night!

Instructions:

Simple: Start and end on an A. Stay within the EZ-Zones and you can't go wrong! Remember, it's your creation, so play whatever YOU feel will sound good.

Advanced: See/hear "Jam Stuff" on the CD for an idea or two. Add some E♭'s and slide into your E's.

Listening Lesson: Listen for the repeated 12 bar phrase. Let your "ear knowledge" of it become second nature and try responding to the end of the phrase by changing what you're doing a bit (maybe play a little less, or more).

Troubleshooting: Don't overthink it! Just play a conversation. ...and don't be afraid to repeat your ideas (and even your so-called mistakes!), because, in music, that's called a motif!

★ ★ ★ ★ ★

P.J. (Post Jam): Tell yourself (or have someone else tell you) that you are the pure embodiment of the blues, and just healed every soul who heard you!

IRISH SEAMAN

Gone to the big city to jam.

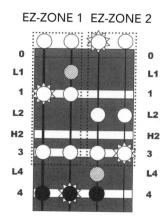

EZ-ZONE 1 EZ-ZONE 2

Jam Stuff: Cut 30

Jam Example: Cut 31

The Way: Three Quarter Time Celtic Rock.

Scale: A Blues.

Key: A minor

Notes: any, A, C, D, E, or G (with E♭'s thrown in for some color).

EZ-Zones: *Low:* 0, 1, 3, on the G and D strings, *and/or, High:* 0, L2, 3, on the A and E strings.

Scale Character: Intensified, serious, and concentrated, but still joyous!

Preparation: Run the EZ-Zone notes up, down, left, right, wrong, inside-out, whatever... until fairly un-thinking.

Instructions:

Simple: Start and end on an A. Stay within the EZ-Zone and you can't go wrong! Remember, it's your creation, so play whatever YOU feel will sound good with the cut.

Advanced: See/hear "Jam Stuff" on the CD for an idea or two. Add E♭'s and slide into your E's. Expand to scale notes outside the EZ-Zone.

Listening Lesson: Notice and respond to the 3/4 meter and accents (three hits) in every 4th bar.

Troubleshooting: Don't get too microscopic. Ride the big waves of inspiration. Just as a sea captain would look ahead out into a storm, watching for coming danger, you should strive to "hear" ahead, listening for where the music and your ideas are leading you.

★ ★ ★ ★ ★

P.J. (Post Jam): Tell yourself (or have someone else tell you) that the concentrated flow you just had was pure liquid inspiration!

STAGEFRIGHT STAGES

OK, you've been jamming with me and the CD for a while now, having some fun, feeling pretty good, and it's about a "no-brainer" to improvise at least within the EZ-Zones. That's Wonderful! You have arrived! Mission accomplished.

But now... The band at cousin Abigale's wedding wants you to sit in! Your whole family knows you've been practicing, and maybe even a select few have been lucky enough to hear you jam a bit in private.

Oh! The Shock! The Horror! The Terror! The Humiliation! The Embarrassment! (need I go on?) How can you bare your very soul to the masses?! Quick! Throw your fiddle in the trash! Hide it (and *you!*) under the bed! Deny that you've ever even *held* one in your now sweaty hands!

Relax. Breath deep. You know that you can improvise just fine. A bit (or even a *lot*) of stagefright is very normal for first timers. Getting over it comes in *stages* (of course! Ha!).

Stage 1:

Fear. "They're all gonna laugh at me!" "What if I stink?" "What if I make a mistake?" "Is my fly open?" "My slip showing?" "A piece of toilet paper stuck to my shoe?" These considerations are all very natural (even if we *know* they're a bit irrational). Just accept it. It's simply part of your first steps. But hey, you're just starting out. How dare they think anything but *positive* thoughts towards your efforts?! Just who do they think they are anyways?! And who appointed *them* your judge and jury?! Go ahead, get a little mad about the situation. It will lead you right to...

Stage 2:

Get Irreverent. Pretend you don't care. The whole audience is just a bunch of ignorant slobs who probably wouldn't know a wrong note if it flew off the end of your bow and bonked them in the head anyways! (Again, not that there even *is* such a thing as a wrong note in improvising). It has helped some (including this author), to imagine that the whole audience is sitting on the *toilet!* (I'll leave the visuals up to you).

Now, you could probably stop right there in your stagefright therapy. Many have. There's not much room for fear when it encounters things like humor and anger. Especially anger. The rock 'n' roll world is full of intense, aloof, and mysterious angry-at-the-world folks. And many times audiences worship these types, I think, mainly because "it" (meaning anger or even any kind of intensity at all!) is something most folks don't get to express in a normal day (or life!) themselves. Which brings us to...

Stage 3:

They need us. Yes, some fears are real. And just maybe your audience is too ignorant to "get it" (and, maybe not). But ultimately, music is a <u>service</u> to the listener and us musicians are the providers of this service... ser<u>vants</u>, if you will. It is also my personal belief that there is more to music than merely sound, and listeners receive more than we may yet know how to measure. With it rides all kinds of feelings and sensations, hopes and dreams (of the listener and performer), even healing, and God knows what else. It is our responsibility and honor to be a conduit for any of these things. Assimilation of this "sacred" stage makes your stagefright journey complete.

THE BOOGIE WOOGIE SECTION

About Boogie Woogie

Unfortunately, we really can't just go "nuts" all the time! (see "Gig Etiquette" on page 38 for more info on this). It may be fun for a while (especially when we are just starting out) and important to get things "under your belt" (or is that under your *fingers?*), but in the end it's just plain boring for the poor audience and other fellow jammers to have one person keep playing and playing and never shut up! It's just like someone who talks too much... and we probably all know someone like this. They talk and talk and talk, and after a while, what they are saying goes in one ear and out the other doesn't it? We stop listening! They're not much fun to play with or be around are they? So, don't be a blabbermouth when you improvise with others!

So, what to do? Does this mean that we must just stand there and listen to others jam as they take their turns? Listening is a ~~good~~... no scratch that, a _great_ thing, but we don't have to necessarily just *stand* there with our finger up our noses either! We just have to simplify a bit and change what we play to a more *supportive* role. The Boogie Woogie (B. W.) pattern is a fun and easy way to accomplish this.

Boogie Woogie is a basic background part that is part of the basics of most of the modern styles of the past 100 years! It's an essential element of jazz, blues, cajun, and anything rock 'n' roll based. To play it for D, G, and A (the 3 most common chords in the key of D), all that we need is *one* finger!... and the ability to bow on two strings at once (I mean on *purpose!* Ha!). You knew that there'd be a catch now didn't ya?

All kidding aside, it's really easy and sounds way-cool too. It's a perfect accompaniment behind vocals and solos of all kinds. See/hear the example called "Zydeco" (page 37, Cuts 39/40) and how I even use it to support the *drums* during their "break." Also, listen to the Fiddle Jam Blues (of course!)
for a real-life example of Boogie Woogie (Cuts 41/42).

Turn the page, and we'll get started with the B. W. Patterns, then on to the Basic, and Fancy B.W. Blues, and a few other tricks and twists before moving on to incorporating it into our jamming (as heard in "Zydeco").

So, let's boogie!...or is that woogie? hmmm...

THE BOOGIE WOOGIE PATTERNS

Here's the basics for the open string based D, G, and A, Boogie Woogie patterns.
<u>Example:</u> Cut 32

The D Boogie Woogie Pattern

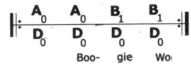

Boo- gie Wo

The G Boogie Woogie Pattern:

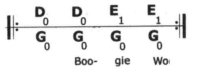

Boo- gie Wo

The A Boogie Woogie Pattern:

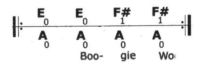

Boo- gie Wo

Helpful Hints:

Bow on two strings at once, but finger only on one string (the higher one). Keep the stoke as straight as you can. If one string stops sounding, simply change the angle of your arm a bit rather than pressing harder to try and force both the strings to meet the bow hairs (this will not be a pleasant sound). As usual, relax and go over it until unthinking. Work up some speed on this (how fast can you go?).

For those who know how to read staff notation, here are the same Boogie Woogie Patterns written out.

Bowing should alternate down and up on each pair of notes. It will sound best if you use just a <u>*little*</u> bow in the upper half. By the way, that's one of the very few times I'll tell anyone to use just a little bow. Usually it will be quite the opposite. For just about everything else, use <u>lots</u> of bow!

THE BASIC B.W. BLUES

Apply the Boogie Woogie patterns in this order to make it into a blues song.
<u>Example:</u> Cut 33

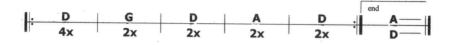

(end on an open D and A together)

Note: D/4x = the D Boogie Woogie pattern played four times non-stop. G/2x = the G pattern two times, etc...Try not to stop between string/pattern changes. Just keep on boogie-ing! Keep it light and easy. Remember, this usually is just a background part.

Watch out! Don't get confused when you get to the last D/2x pattern before repeating, there are four (4) *more* D's coming (that's D/6x's all together) when you reach the beginning again! I've heard *professional* bands get mixed up there before! It's not so hard if you concentrate a bit and don't forget to *count* though. Just stay sharp and keep it flowing.

...and, for those who are "staff conscious," here's the same thing written out.

The Basic Boogie Woogie Blues in the key of D

THE "FANCY" B.W. BLUES
Example: Cut 34

This one *seems* longer and more difficult at first, but most folks find it actually easier once they get the hang of it. It *is* twice as long as the Basic B.W. Blues, but you are probably getting better and better each time you play the Boogie Woogies, so therefore can do this one at a faster tempo (speed) now, taking less time. Also, this one moves around a bit more (especially towards the end) making it easier to follow by ear because it doesn't have so many long stretches of the same pattern repeating.

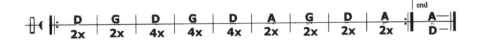

(end on an open D and A)

Like it? You can actually sit in with most any band and play this! They won't know what a "fancy" blues is (that's just a term I made up for you and I in this book only), but they most probably will know exactly what you are about to play if you said, "Guys! Follow me! 12 bar blues in D! From the top!" and then count it off and proceed to play, letting them filter in as they get in sync with you (which my not be until the last bar or two, but that doesn't matter. Just don't let it throw you off).

...and again, for the "staff conscious," here's the same thing written out.

The"Fancy" Boogie Woogie Blues in the key of D
Note: Cut 34 - as written. Cut 36 - ♫ - ♪♪ (see page 35)

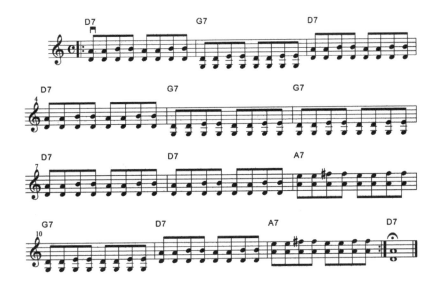

Now we get to the *really* cool stuff!

SHUFFLE RHYTHM * (my personal favorite)
Example: Cut 35

*Note: Shuffle Rhythm is not to be confused with shuffle _bowing_ from old-time fiddling style music which is many times taught as "potato-potato," "run pony-run pony" or, "grasshopper-grasshopper" in beginning violin classes or, staff-wise:

What we've done up to this point in the Boogie Woogie Section examples has all been what's called "straight" rhythm. Each syllable and note was exactly the same length in metronomic precision. Written on the staff, it is generally represented by eighth notes:

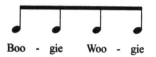

(see page 33, "Fancy Boogie Woogie" as an example).

If I was to explain "straight" rhythm in more visual terms, it would look like this:

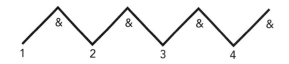

The switch to **shuffle rhythm** is a subtle change to a long-short, long-short alternation. Now… before I explain it further, I should say that as a teacher, I'm more apt to "trick" the unwary student into a shuffle rhythm at this point than explain it to death. I find it comes pretty naturally to most students just by _hearing_ it first, so I'll direct you to listen to Cut 35 on the CD before we go any further.

…cool huh?

Run the cut again, but play along this time, using only a repeated D boogie woogie pattern. Notice how the rhythm gradually shifted from "straight" at the beginning, to a more "bouncy" one at the end of the cut. The difference is subtle, but dramatic in the _feel_ department.

OK, now, mentally you'll need to clearly <u>understand</u> the difference between them to be able to recall it later at will.

Technically, the change from straight to shuffle rhythm is based on dividing each beat into **three** segments (usually called "triplets"). We <u>elongate</u> the first note, "boo-" or "woo-" of boogie woogie, (usually a _down_ bow) to approximately cover 2/3rds of the beat (instead of 1/2 as it was in the straight version), then <u>shorten</u> the second note a bit, the "-gie's," (and, usually a quick _up_ bow) to somewhere around insert the remaining 1/3rd of the beat.

> *Notice that I just used the words "approximately" and "somewhere around." Stylistic variations to this rhythm are the <u>norm</u> rather than the exception. Sometimes players "flatten out" the rhythm to be somewhere in-between straight and shuffle. Jazz and Blues influenced musics are famous for this shifting of the rhythmic feel depending on the tune, tempo, or even whim of the performer, but you'll find variations of this sort in nearly every style of music (yes, even Classical).

Try to use the same amounts of bow for both the down and up strokes, even though they are different lengths of time, or else you'll gradually run out of bow! Keep it light, in the upper half, with loose and flexible finger and wrist joints. You probably won't need to use more than 2 or 3 inches (5 - 8 cm.) of the hair.

The result should be a little more of a loose and "loopy" feel. Visually I represent this as:

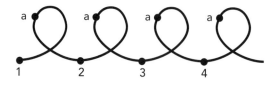

Can you "see" it?

Shuffle rhythm **notation** is the tricky part. To write it out literally (not that that it is always even *possible* because of the variations mentioned above) is quite a mess to look at...unsightly triplet brackets all over the place or, in 12/8 time, which makes it even *harder* to visually differentiate where the beats are ("the beat" being a pretty important thing to these styles I think)...It all tends to make it confusing for such a natural *sounding* thing. As I mention elsewhere in this book (page 40), music is sound and feeling, and not just dots and squiggles on a page, so musicians have come up with a nifty little way to direct us when to shuffle the rhythm: that is mostly...change nothing! ...except mentally note one little "secret" mark at the beginning of a song or section:

That's it! Music writers find it far better to simply write music as "easy-on-the-eyes" straight 8th notes and tell the performer to **interpret** it as a triplet-based rhythm. The result is much clearer (which would be you sounding cool and flowing, rather than stiff and boring!).

So, whenever you see this "two-eighths-equals-a-quarter-and-eighths-note-triplet-figure" thing-y, shuffle away!

Further style clarification: "Shuffle feel" and, I should add, its famous cousin "swing feel," (which, by the way, are words you may also sometimes see written with, or instead of the above symbol), is loosely based on dividing each beat by 3, and "straight feel" is divided equally by 2. These two basic "feels" divide about ALL music of ALL styles and eras into about a 50/50 split! It's almost always one or the other.

Can you name some styles and whether they are generally a "divided by 2" or "divided by 3" kind of rhythm? There are examples of both on your Fiddle Jam CD. Check out Cuts: 11, 17, 19, 23, 29, 36, 42, and 44 for examples of shuffle/swing ("3" based rhythms), and Cuts: 3, 5, 7, 9, 13, 15, 21, 25, 27, 31, 33, 34, 38, and 40 for examples of straight ("2" based rhythms).

Fancy B.W. Blues - Shuffle
<u>Example</u>: Cut 36

OK, now that we have experienced what shuffle rhythm is (pages 34 – 35), lets *use* it!

Simply return to page 33 for the "Fancy" Boogie Woogie progression and notations, but this time reinterpret the written rhythm to shuffle as you play along with Cut 36 (instead of Cut 34).

Remember: ♫ = ♩♪ simply means to play music written as normal 8th notes (which is much easier to look at), as shuffle rhythm/style instead. That's it! In this case, it's thankfully easier <u>done</u> than <u>said</u>! So don't think too much. OK?

Have fun, and then meet me back on page 36 for the next Boogie Woogie twist...Low 2!

THE "LOW 2" BOOGIE WOOGIE PATTERNS

Example: Cut 37

OK, now here's a twist that will add a little spice to your boogie! This one adds... you guessed it: the *lowered second finger* to the mix.

The Low 2 Boogie Woogie Pattern starts out just like the original Boogie Woogie Pattern (back on page 31), but then keeps going, past the first finger, on to low 2, and back to 1, before repeating. Try it for D, G, and A, individually before putting them all together in the Low 2 B. W. Blues progression on page 36.

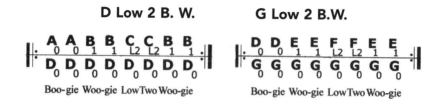

...and the same written in staff notation:

THE "LOW 2" BOOGIE WOOGIE BLUES

Example: Cut 38

Use the Low 2 Patterns (above) in this progression. Notice that the order is the same as the "Fancy" B.W. Blues (page 33), but since the Low 2 pattern is twice as long as the original Boogie Woogie pattern (page 31), each one is repeated half as many times as before.

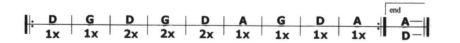

(end on an open D and A)

Cool huh? This one should sound the most "moving" of the three Boogie Woogies we've learned so far. Maybe because it *does* move more for one reason (of course! Ha!), but also partly because the lowered 2nd finger notes seem to linger in our minds, leading our ears to the next chord more easily too. Keep the rhythm flowing to help this feeling even more. Always try to listen ahead in your mind to "hear" the next chord change coming and make a smooth transition right into it.

The Low 2 B.W. Blues staff notation

(just in case you need it)

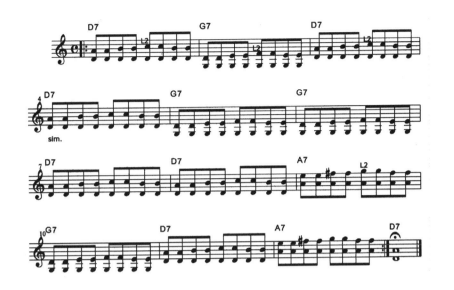

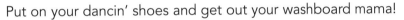

P.J. (Pre Jam): by the way: as an extra bonus, you can also jam over this and all other Boogie Woogie Cuts (33-38) using the D Blues Scale! See page 41 for the D Blues fingering chart.

ZYDECO

Put on your dancin' shoes and get out your washboard mama!

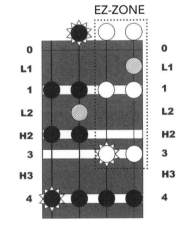

EZ-ZONE

Jam Stuff: Cut 39

Jam Example: Cut 40

The Low-Down: Boogie Woogie cajun meets Rock n Roll in the swamps 'roun' "N'orlan, Lueezian" (New Orleans, Louisiana).

Scale: D Major Pentatonic.

Key: D Major.

Notes: any, D, E, F#, A, or, B (with some F naturals thrown in for extra color).

EZ-Zone: 0, 1, 3, on the A and E strings.

(Notice how this EZ-Zone is identical to B Blues [see cuts: 39, and 40], except D is now the new "tonic" note and not B).

Scale Character: Country-cool, upbeat, but still with a bluesy tang.

Preparation: Run the EZ-Zone notes any which way that pleases you until fairly un-thinking, getting used to D being the new "tonic."

Instructions:

Simple: Start and end on a D, stay within the EZ-Zone, and you can't go wrong! Remember, it's your creation, so play whatever YOU feel will sound good with the cut.

Advanced: See/hear "Jam Stuff" on the CD for an idea or two. Add some F naturals and slide into your F#'s. Expand to scale notes outside the EZ-Zone. Concentrate on hearing, trusting, and obeying your inner ideas.

Listening Lesson: Notice the drum/fiddle breaks, and syncopated snare drum beat. How will you respond to it? (see troubleshooting)

Troubleshooting: Don't freak out in the drum breaks. Stay focused, confident, and flowing (it may help you to imagine the rest of the band still playing).

★ ★ ★ ★ ★

P.J. (Post Jam): Tell yourself (or have someone else tell you) that that was true greatness. Directly channeled from the Swamp Gods!

"Geoff and Jimi"
"Turning Up The Heat"

Original photograph of Jimi Hendrix © Jim Marshall 1967, 1995®

Photo image by Dan Syracuse/Big Bang Graphics

Wit & Wisdom

"GIG ETIQUETTE AND THE REAL WORLD"

Getting the chance to **"sit in"** with a band can be a real "shot in the arm" as they say, and it need not be filled with fear and loathing if you just understand a few simple things about how these situations usually work.

First off, music is very much like conversation. Remember, nobody wants to listen to a blabbermouth for very long, or someone who repeats themselves endlessly, so don't take too many **"choruses"** (see "about boogie woogie" page 30). Take the turn given to you and get out of the way musically, and maybe physically too if it's a small and cramped stage and don't play anything but complimentary and supportive background things while someone else is "soloing" (like Boogie Woogie). It's also pretty tiring to listen to someone who speaks (or plays) too soft, or too loud for any length of time (see below about adjusting volume and tone).

Remember, **balance is everything**. Breathe deep, take it easy. Push when you feel the need, and lay back when appropriate too. Always listen inside your own mind (you know that that's where the best stuff is always going to be, so just give in and trust it!).

Next, get your equipment in order as quickly as you can when it's time for you to come up and play. Keep it simple. If you're playing electric, don't go crazy with too many effects that will take a long time to set up. One instrument, one chord, straight into the amp (yours preferably) will make for a quick and efficient set up and will probably be most appreciated by the band, who has been kind enough to let you take part in a tune or two on their **"gig"**. Going direct into their **PA system** is even simpler ("PA" stands for Public Address by the way), but usually leaves you with inferior results in sound and control in these situations. You may end up too loud, or too soft and feel like a self-conscious pain if asking for adjustments to your sound.

Getting the right **volume** is critical to a good performance. Set your volume as close as you can to what you think will be equal to the other instruments. Then, don't be afraid to tactfully play a note or two (hopefully one that harmonizes) as the band starts the tune if the opportunity is there, and stop to adjust your sound further if necessary. Again, try to do all this quickly, confidently, and efficiently as possible, because you may not have as much of a chance to further adjust once the tune gets going (and all eyes and ears are on *you* we hope!).

Try to be quick about adjusting your **tone** too (not as much of a problem if you are using your own amp, but very important if going direct into a strange PA!). Too treble-y, just like too loud (see "a Sound Environment," page 9), will make you hold back too much and lose bow control. Turning up the "bass" or "Low EQ" control a bit ("EQ" = equalization) is usually a safe bet for the violin, and will tend to round the sound out in a rather pleasing way.

Don't forget to **tune up** of course! Check your tuning with someone in the band, or tune with an electronic tuner beforehand.

Other than that, your **mental state** is most important! Try not to think (you know that by now), just concentrate on *listening* to both: outer (you and the rest of the band), and inner (your own ideas as they come in *response* to the band). It's a split-brain state of mind that may take years to get consistent with, so don't be too dismayed if you get distracted at times! You'll eventually earn/learn to ignore anything (including your own mental anxieties) except what you "hear" to play, and emote!

If you are in the situation where there is a band leader (or someone who is kind of helping you), keep an eye on him/her (especially as a phrase comes to an end) for some **visual clues** as to what is going to happen next. Remember this is jamming we're talking about here, so things get made up as we go, including song lengths and forms.

A soloist finishing a **"chorus"** may look at you to "hand off" the next solo to, or look toward the band leader to signal that they are finishing. It's OK if you don't start right on the down beat for your solo. It might be best to wait for applause for the previous solo to die down anyways (if any), and/or sometimes a bit of silence is simply "golden."

Someone in the band pointing to their head (after the solos or an elongated intro) usually means, the band is proceeding to the **"head"** (or melody). Keep your ears and eyes open when nearing the end of a song too. They may add a **"tag"** (a repeat of the last phrase a few times), or **"ritard"** (gradually slowing down) at the end and hold out the last note a bit (called a **"fermatta"**). Stay sharp and keep one eye on the drummer, if there is one, for that.

Attitude. If you're too pushy and bold (usually not a problem for a slightly nervous beginning jammer), don't expect the band to keep you up for very many songs, let alone, ask you to sit in again! And of course, don't expect to be paid for just sitting in either.

Remember, it's their **gig**, so be humble, respectful, and professional, and most of all, thankful for the chance to experience jamming live and in the real world!

THE "TUNE" SECTION

Just as promised *way* back in the beginning of this book (see "Q & A's" on page 4, "What You Can Expect..."), I will include a couple of tunes or songs for your enjoyment. This book, as you hopefully understand by now, is not about *songs,* (there are literally thousands of good books on the market already about that!), but, this book *is* about improvising over, or with, songs though, so, I figure including a couple will do the student no harm whatsoever.

I find that most violinists already know how to read standard staff notation or "music" as it is usually, although, mistakenly called, in my opinion (see note * below). So, I have chosen to include two fun songs I've composed for students, written out in standard notation. For those who do not yet know how to read "music," I will also include as many "helps" as possible (like: fingerings and note names). Whether you know how to read or not, I highly recommend listening to the recordings *first.* Maybe even going so far as to try to figure out the melodies without the notation in this book!

* Note: It is firmly my opinion that what we usually call written music is not really music at all. The dots, lines, and squiggles we call "music" are merely *notation* to help and guide us in making a desired sound.

It is excellent ear and mental training to do this sort of work. If you're bold enough to try and up for a challenge, I recommend a quick finger on the pause button. By this I mean, stop the recording as often as you need (even every note!).

There is absolutely no shame in figuring it out one note at a time. Yes, it is true that some people have a natural ability to hear something once and then be able to repeat it (wouldn't that be handy?), but that doesn't mean that that person will end up being a better musician than you. The important thing is to *learn,* so don't get discouraged if it takes you a while.

Music is the sound we make and the feelings we project through, because of, and with it.

A drawing of a house is not a house. Written words do not make a lesson. Only the meaning of the words understood is a lesson. We must all be careful not to confuse the two. Keep your attention on the sound you make and the feeling it gives you and others. This approach will lead to much happiness and satisfaction.

"Tune" Section Contents

First is **THE FIDDLE JAM BLUES** (of course!) on page 41.
It uses just the first and third fingers, similar to a blues scale. Watch out for the proper first fingers though. Sometimes they are regular 1 (B1 and F#1), and other times a Low 1 will be needed (L1 F natural).

Second is **THE BOUNCY BLUES** on page 42. It was named by a student who thought it sounded, well..."bouncy" (again, of course!). This one is a little trickier so watch out! Enjoy.

THE FIDDLE JAM BLUES

OK, lets put it *ALL* together now.

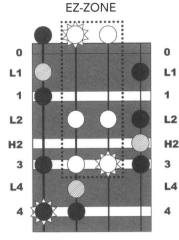

EZ-ZONE

Jam Stuff: Cut 41

Jam Example: Cuts 42

In Tune: Three in one. A simple melody, jamming, and Boogie Woogie example.

Scale: D Blues.

Key: D "universal" (major notes in chords and minor notes in the scale).

Jamming Notes: any, D, F, G, A, or C, with some A♭'s thrown in for color.

EZ-Zone: 0, L2, 3, on the D and A strings.

Scale Character: excited with a slight mean streak.

Preparation (for improvisation): Run the EZ-Zone notes up and down, inside out and sideways until fairly un-thinking.**Instructions (for improvisation):**
Simple: Start and end on a D, stay within the EZ-Zone, and you can't go wrong! Remember, it's *your* creation, so play whatever *YOU* feel will sound good with the cut.

Advanced: See/hear "Jam Stuff" on the CD for an idea or two. Add A♭'s and slide into your A's. Expand to scale notes outside the EZ-Zone.

Preparation (for playing the melody): 1) Just wander through the notes, one at a time, to get them correct. Learn them either by stopping and starting the CD for each new note, by applying the note names and fingerings provided on the chart (notice that there are only 0's, 1's, and 3's), or, by simply reading the chart itself (preferred if you know how), or, better yet, "All-of-the above." 2) *Without* your instrument, tap or clap the rhythm to the melody along with the CD until confident that you know it. 3) Now, extra slow and without the *CD*, put the correct notes in the correct order with the correct timing. Then speed it up gradually each time until you can play it along with the CD. Easier said than done as they say, but I find that separating it into "practice parts" (notes, rhythm, and tempo) usually can complete the learning process in less time than just sort of having a "go" at it and hoping for the best. Repetition has its merits for sure, but if you don't learn the parts correctly to begin with, and keep playing the same mistakes over and over, you're guaranteed to become one thing...*an expert mistake maker!* Take the time to get it right. It's well worth the effort.

Preparation (for the Boogie Woogie accompaniment):
It's just a "fancy" L2 boogie woogie pattern and form/order (see page 36).

Listening Lesson: Can you pick out all three parts (melody, boogie woogie, and jamming) and when each starts and/or stops? Listen to the CD without playing, imagining yourself playing one of the parts the whole way through.

Troubleshooting: It gets a bit chaotic toward the end (and isn't that cool?!). Keep your attention on the drum part and the Boogie Woogie if you find yourself losing the feel of the beat. As a musician, you must cultivate the ability to stay concentrated on this most basic element no matter how crazy the parts around it get!

★ ★ ★ ★ ★

P.J. (Post Jam): Tell yourself (or have someone else tell you) that you are like the Buddha of jamming and the flow master of flow for the way you can hold yourself together amidst musical mayhem!

The Fiddle Jam Blues staff notation chart

By:G.F.Perry

THE BOUNCY BLUES

Named by a student because, well...it sounded "bouncy!"

Jam Stuff: Cut 43

Jam Example: Cut 44

In the Mood: Follow the bouncing ball!

Scale: A Blues.

Key: A "universal" (major notes in the melody and chords, and minor notes in the blues scale).

Notes: any, A, C, D, E, or G (with E♭'s thrown in for extra color).

EZ-Zone(s): *Low:* 0, 1, 3, on the G and D strings, *and/or, High:* 0, L2, 3, on the A and E strings.

Scale Character: Bold and sassy, but still in a happy and bouncy sort of way (of course!).

Preparation (for improvisation): Run the EZ-Zone(s) notes up and down, sideways, inside-out, etc...until fairly un-thinking.

Instructions (for improvisation):

Simple: Start and end on an A, stay within the EZ-Zone(s), and you can't go wrong! Remember, it's your creation, so play whatever *YOU* feel will sound good with the cut.

Advanced: See/hear "Jam Stuff" on the CD for an idea or two. Add E♭'s and slide into your E's. Pay some attention to connecting the two EZ-Zones seamlessly.

Preparation (for the melody/tune): Look it over. Listen to the cut. Learn the correct notes first (not worrying about the rhythm right away). Then, without your instrument, learn the rhythm by counting and tapping or clapping it out before applying the notes. Then lastly, and extra slow at first, put the correct notes with the correct rhythm, slow enough so that you can play it perfectly without even flinching. Speed it up a little more each time you practice it until up to the tempo of the CD example. Again, separating it into parts seems like the long way to learn, but I've found we get to the desired end result (knowing the tune well) faster, and in the end, better, than by just sort of "wanging" at it over and over again *hoping* it will get better!

Practice Motto: fix your mistakes right away or you'll just become an *"expert mistake maker!"*

Listening Lesson: Notice the shuffle rhythm (paying particular attention to the cymbals and snare drum). Doesn't it have a looping, more circular motion than plain straight 8th note music? Shuffle-based music may seem a bit choppy to the ear at first, but really does (or at least *should*) have a "rounded, rolling, slightly lop-sided" flow to it.

Troubleshooting: Continuing from the listening lesson above, don't let your shuffle rhythm feel get too stiff and mechanical. Just roll with it like little ripples on a bigger wave. Our theme: "Don't think (too much), just do." Technically, keep it light and near the tip of the bow, using... and again, this is one of the very few times you will hear me tell you this (usually it's just the opposite)...just a little bow (no more than 2 or 3 inches/5-8cm). Start down bow on the down beat and give the shorter upstroke a flick of the fingers (especially the index) on your bow hand.

★ ★ ★ ★ ★

P.J. (Post Jam): Tell yourself (or have someone else tell you) that what you just jammed to this example gave your/their life a new and happy meaning!

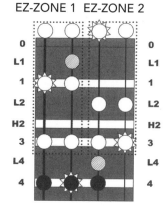

The Bouncy Blues staff notation chart

"Closing in On the path to Nirvana"

(no, not the band, I mean the place of bliss within your own soul!)

Well, I hope that I've helped you to get started on the path to rock n roll improvising! May it bring you a lifetime of fiddle jamming joy!

Never forget that the greatest ideas are already "there," ripe for the plucking. Whether they are "out" there or "in" there (meaning your mind), is no matter, for all that we have to do is relax, listen, and respond!

Happy Jamming,

Geoffrey Fitzhugh Perry

"The Path"

Photo image by Dan Syracuse/Big Bang Graphics

CREDITS

All compositions and arrangements by:

Geoffrey Fitzhugh Perry

Violin (and a few guitar, bass, and keyboard overdubs) played and recorded by G. F. Perry

The Boys in the band:

Paul Campanella Jr.: Drums
Aaron Flynt: Guitar
Aaron Trubic: Bass

Studio Engineer for band tracks: John Caruso

Recorded at: Audio Magic, Buffalo, NY, USA

Assembled and Mastered at: The Digital Visionary Recording Studio, www.thedigitalvisionary.com

Cover artwork and direction: Bob Campbell and Staff at Campbell Associates, Orchard Park, NY

Digital Images: Dan Syracuse, Big Bang Graphics, Williamsville, NY

Final Layout Design: Mari Anderson, Lights On Graphics, www.LightsOnGraphics.com

THANK YOU'S

My wife Elizabeth for her love (and for keeping me on track).

My friends and families for their encouragement.

Dale Anderson for believing in me enough to plunk his hard-earned cash down towards the studio production of this product.

Stewart Shapiro, Bob Goods, and the law associates at Cohen and Lambardo for legal advice.

Ryan Dee and Al Monti for computer layout help.

Jack Kulp of Digital Visionary for data storage help.

Mark Panfil for school sales advice.

Jessie Weaver for his enthusiasm and help in promotion.

Mark Mazur for being a sounding board.

Paul Carrol Binkley for his sincere interest, encouragement, friendship and advice on things NOT to do.

Jon, Roseanne, and Roy Payne for their encouragement, time, energy, and support.

Vicki Smith for her proofreading expertise.

Barb Perry for the costumes seen in the Fiddle Jam photos.

Phil Georger of Hamburg Music Center, Hamburg, NY for use of electronic piano.

Arts Council of Buffalo for providing invaluable legal advice, free-of-charge!

All my students (and parents), past and present, for putting up with my weekly stories, and for whom without, this book would not have existed.

Mari Anderson, Lights On Graphics, www.LightsOnGraphics.com for her patient diligence in the original 1st printing layout design.

FIDDLE JAM CONTACT INFORMATION

Fiddle Jamming questions or comments can be directed to Geoffrey Fitzhugh Perry via the internet at:

www.fiddlejam.com

This Fiddle Jam page is part of the author's main site: **www.fanaticalfitzhugh.com**

Watch these sites (and/or sign up on the fiddle jam email list!) for future updates on other books, recordings, and fiddle jam related products, services, and general jam stuff like:

1) **The (free!) "Fiddle Jam interactive Song Key Archive."** Search, request, and/or post what scale to use to jam along with your favorite recordings! Teachers! Contact us about becoming a moderator for this site feature!

2) **Fiddle Jam Clinics:** Have Geoff or an associate come to your school or organization to teach you the fiddle jammin' ways directly!

3) **"Art Fitzhugh" hand painted instruments!** Wild and fun! Great for stage or just inspiration. The embodiment of the attitudes expressed in this book.

4) **String Orchestra Scores and Charts** for the Fiddle Jam Blues and the Bouncy Blues (and others to come soon!).

5) **Educational Publications:** "Fiddle Jam for Teachers" and "Fiddle Jam for parents," are upcoming, along with other publications (some as free downloads!).

About the Author

Classically and jazz trained, rock 'n' roll schooled, award winning, multi-instrumentalist, Geoffrey Fitzhugh Perry, has developed into a world class master improviser and educator through his diverse experiences in nearly all imaginable styles of music over the past 20 plus years as a professional.

A D'Addario String Endorsing Artist, Geoff is most noted thus far for his work with the virtuosic instrumental rock group Gamalon (www.gamalon.com) who's MCA/Amherst Records highlights include a #8 Billboard Jazz Chart showing, and recording and touring with sax great Ernie Watts, he has also recorded and toured with Nashville New-Age guitarist Paul Carrol Binkley (www.heartdancemusic.com), has appeared as Buffalo Sabres "Fiddleman!", and released two solo recordings as Fitzhugh and the Fanatics, "Blue Standards" and "Flavor" (on the HotWings Entertainment label).

Born, raised, and currently residing in the Buffalo, NY area with wife Elizabeth, he remains an in-demand part of the music community there, retaining a full roster of private students, a String Orchestra post at the Aurora Waldorf School, does stringed instrument demonstrations/performances in schools as part of "The Stringmen" (with guitarist Doug Yeomans), Fiddle Jam clinics, and is a member of many area groups including: LeeRon Zydeco and the Hot Tamales (www.LeeRon.com), and Emery Nash. (www.emerynash.com).

CD Index

Cut#	Lesson	page	Scale	Violin EZ-Zone fingering
1	Tuning Notes			
2 & 3	The Raven's Daughter	(10)	G Major	0,1,h2,3, on G & D
4 & 5	Le Bomb	(11)	A Major	0,1,h2,3, on A & E
6 & 7	Spiral Travels	(13)	A Major	0,1,h2,3, on A & E
8 & 9	The Rarest Rose	(14)	G Major	0,1,h2,3, on G & D
10 & 11	Cajun Waltz	(15)	D Major	0,1,h2,3, on D & A
12 & 13	Contra Dance	(16)	D Major	0,1,h2,3, on D & A
14 & 15	E Funki	(18)	E Blues	0,1,3, on D & A
16 & 17	E12	(18)	E Blues	0,1,3, on D & A
18 & 19	B. Tuff.	(20)	B Blues	0,1,3, on A & E
20 & 21	B. Gone	(21)	B Blues	0,1,3, on A & E
22 & 23	G Swing	(23)	G Blues	0,L2,3, on G & D
24 & 25	Moon Diggin'	(24)	G Blues	0,L2,3, on G & D
26 & 27	A Potter's Wheel	(26)	A Blues	0,1,3, on G & D, _and_ 0,L2,3, on A & E
28 & 29	Blue Suit in a Road-house Bar of 12	(27)	A Blues	(same as above)
30 & 31	Irish Seaman	(28)	A Blues	(same as above)
32	B.W. Patterns	(31)	★	(notation)
33	Basic B.W. Blues	(32)	★	(notation)
34	Fancy B.W. Blues	(33)	★	(notation)
35	Straight vs. Shuffle	(34)	★	(graphics)
36	Fancy B.W. Blues-Shuffle	(35)	★	(notation)
37	L2 B.W. Patterns	(36)	★	(notation)
38	L2 B.W. Blues	(36)	★	(notation)
39 & 40	Zydeco	(37)	D Maj. Pent.	0,1,3, on A & E
41 & 42	The Fiddle Jam Blues	(41)	D Blues	0,L2,3, on D & A
43 & 44	The Bouncy Blues	(42)	A Blues	(see 26 & 27 above)

Note: This CD features a "Split Track" Mix. Jam along with Geoff on the
Left channel (with Band), and go it alone (Band only) on the Right channel.

Learn To Play Today

with folk music instruction from

Hal Leonard Banjo Method

Authored by Mac Robertson, Robbie Clement & Will Schmid. This innovative method teaches 5-string, bluegrass style. The method consists of two instruction books and two cross-referenced supplement books that offer the beginner a carefully-paced and interest-keeping approach to the bluegrass style.

Method Book 1
00699500 Book $6.95
00695101 Book/CD Pack $16.95

Method Book 2
00699502 ....$6.95

Supplementary Songbooks
00699515 Easy Banjo Solos $6.95
00699516 More Easy Banjo Solos $6.95

Hal Leonard Dulcimer Method
by Neal Hellman

A beginning method for the Appalachian dulcimer with a unique new approach to solo melody and chord playing. Includes tuning, modes and many beautiful folk songs all demonstrated on the audio accompaniment. Music and tablature.
00699289 Book $6.95
00697230 Book/CD Pack $14.95

Teach Yourself To Play The Folk Harp
by Sylvia Woods

This is the first book written exclusively for the folk harp that teaches the student how to play the instrument, step by step. Each of the 12 lessons includes instructions, exercises and folk and classical pieces using the new skills and techniques taught in the lesson. This is an excellent book for any student, regardless of previous musical training.
00722251 Book $12.95
00722252 Cassette $7.95
00722253 Video...$54.95

The Hal Leonard Mandolin Method

Noted mandolinist and teacher Rich Del Grosso has authored this excellent mandolin method that features play-along audio duets, great playable tunes in several styles (bluegrass, country, folk, blues), and standard music notation and tablature.
00699296 Book $6.95
00695102 Book/CD Pack $14.95

Jumpin' Jim's Ukulele Tips 'N' Tunes
A Beginner's Method and Songbook

This fantastic book for ukulele includes: Amazing Grace • Aura Lee • Bill Bailey, Won't You Please Come Home • (Oh, My Darling) Clementine • Give My Regards to Broadway • He's Got the Whole World in His Hands • Home on the Range • I've Been Working on the Railroad • Let Me Call You Sweetheart • My Country, 'Tis of Thee (America) • Oh! Susanna • She'll Be Comin' 'Round the Mountain • The Star Spangled Banner • Swing Low, Sweet Chariot • When the Saints Go Marching In • You're a Grand Old Flag • and more.
00699406 Ukulele Technique $12.95

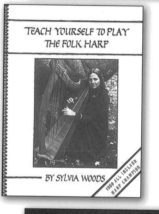

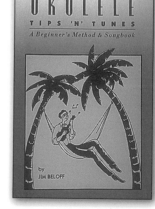

FOR MORE INFORMATION, SEE YOUR LOCAL MUSIC DEALER, OR WRITE TO:

HAL•LEONARD®
CORPORATION
7777 W. BLUEMOUND RD. P.O. BOX 13819 MILWAUKEE, WI 53213

Visit Hal Leonard Online at
www.halleonard.com

Prices and availability subject to change without notice.